2024 Vision board
CLIP ART BOOK

ACCUMULATE EXPERIENCE

FINANCIAL SAVINGS

FINANCIAL INVESTMENT

FACTS!

REAL!

BEST!

FRESH!

www.

PROFITABLE!

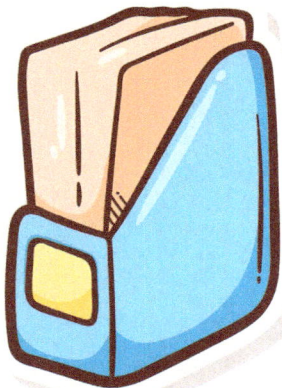

SUCCESS

REASONABLE SPENDING

Rick

SAVE THE MONEY

FINANCIAL MANAGEMENT

STOCK INVESTMENT

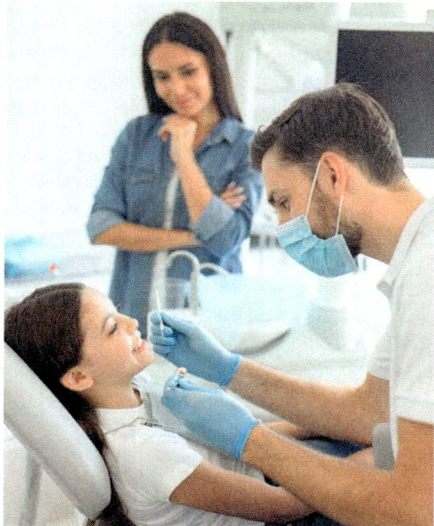

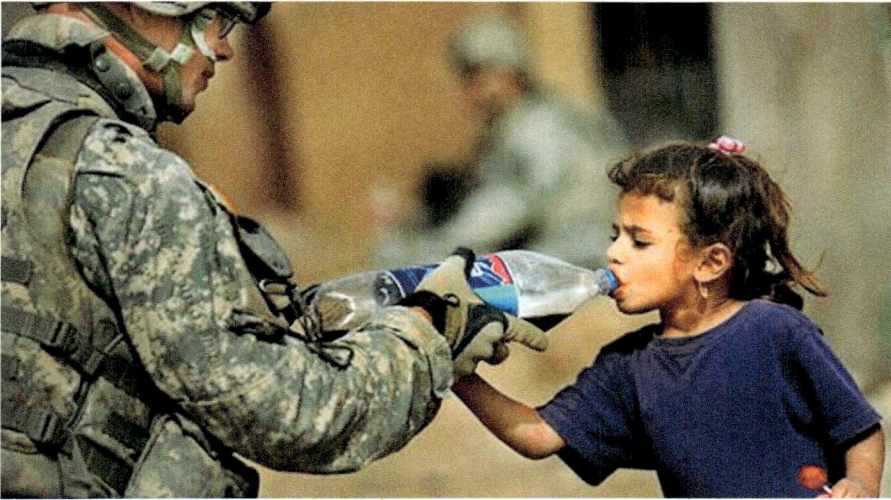

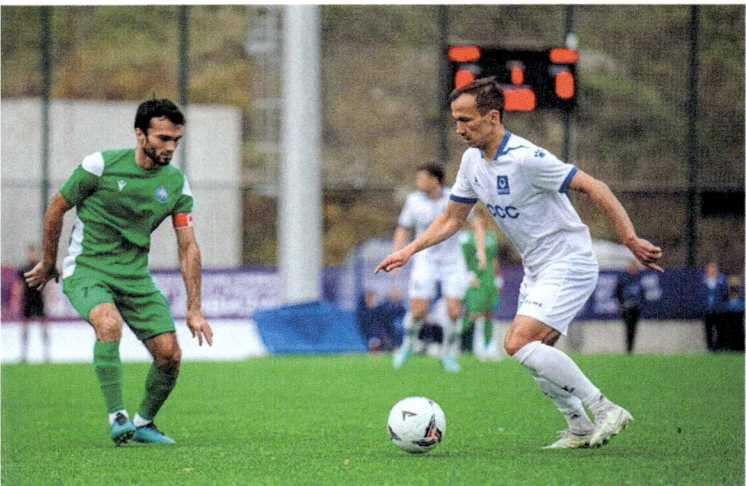

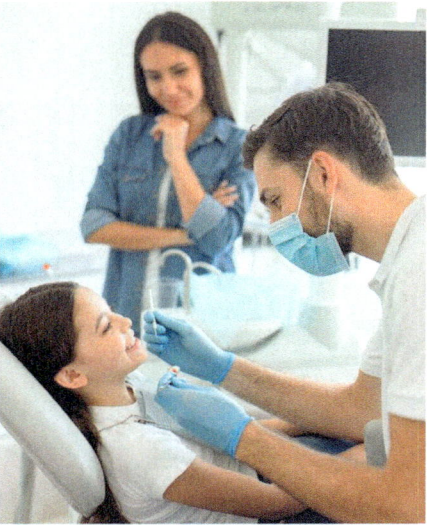

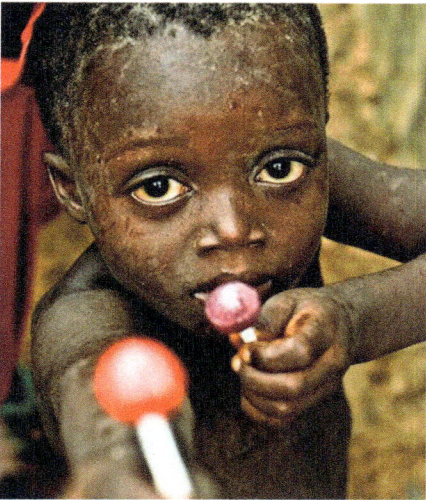

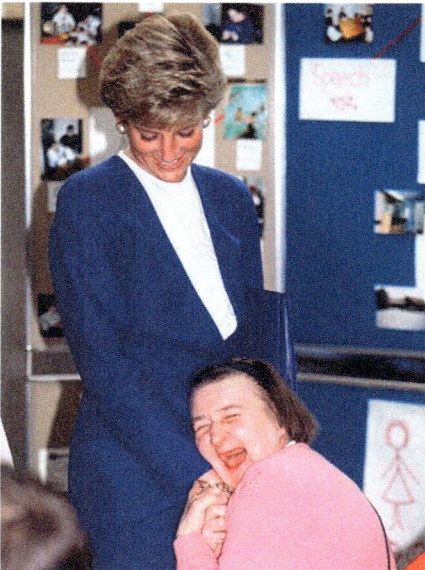

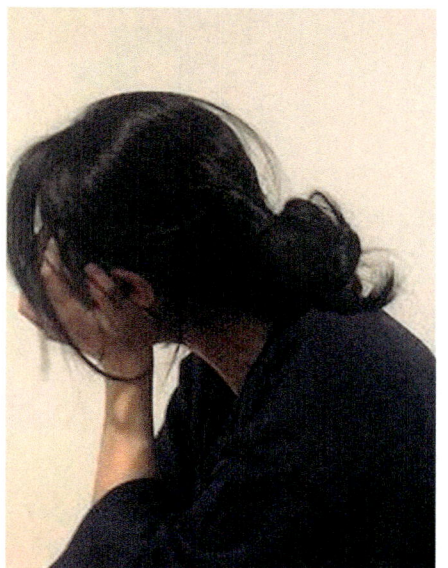

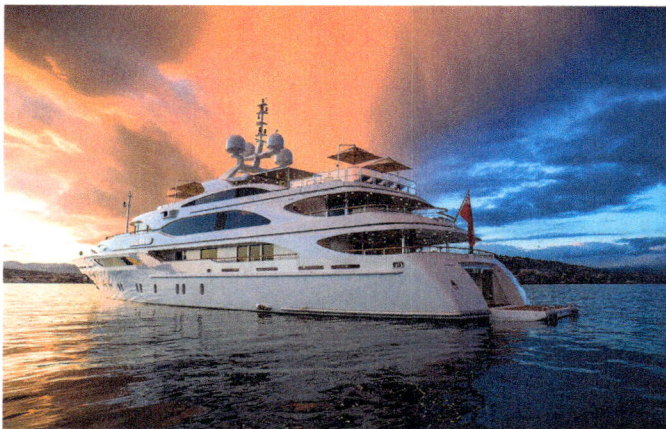

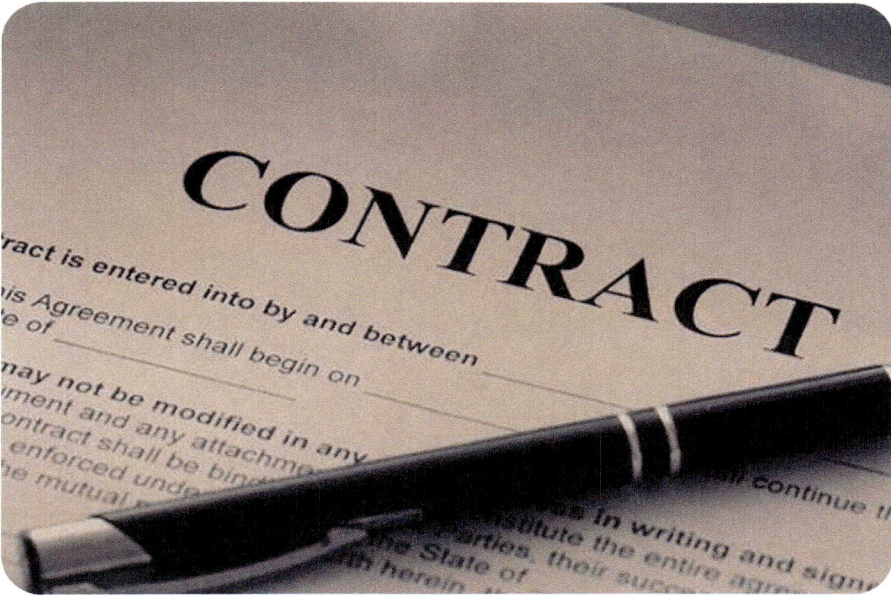

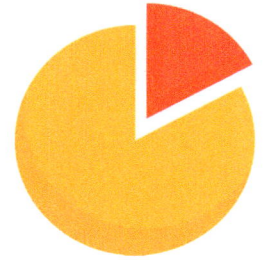

MONEY

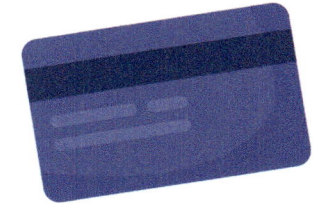

PAY ✓

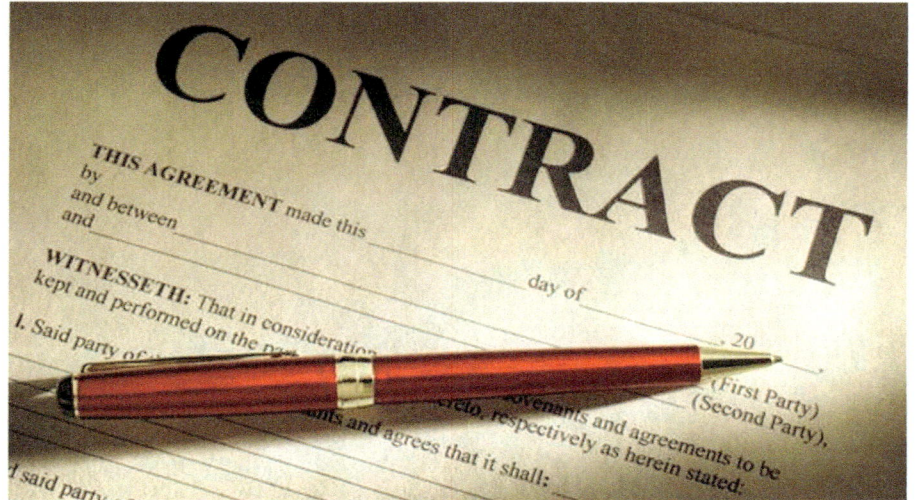

Printed in Great Britain
by Amazon